Sofie's S Book

WRITTEN BY **J. L. MAZZEO**
ILLUSTRATED BY **HELEN ROSS REVUTSKY**

dingles & company New Jersey

First Printing

Published By dingles&company
P.O. Box 508
Sea Girt, New Jersey 08750

LIBRARY OF CONGRESS CATALOG CARD NUMBER
2005907289

ISBN
ISBN-13: 978 1-59646-524-4
ISBN-10: 1-59646-524-7

Printed in the United States of America

My Letter Library series is based on the
original concept of Judy Mazzeo Zocchi.

ART DIRECTION
Barbie Lambert & Rizco Design
DESIGN
Rizco Design
EDITED BY
Andrea Curley
PROJECT MANAGER
Lisa Aldorasi
EDUCATIONAL CONSULTANT
Maura Ruane McKenna
PRE-PRESS BY
Pixel Graphics

**EXPLORE THE LETTERS OF THE ALPHABET
WITH MY LETTER LIBRARY***
Aimee's **A** Book
Bebe's **B** Book
Cassie's **C** Book
Delia's **D** Book
Emma's **E** Book
Faye's **F** Book
George's **G** Book
Henry's **H** Book
Izzy's **I** Book
Jade's **J** Book
Kelsey's **K** Book
Logan's **L** Book
Mia's **M** Book
Nate's **N** Book
Owen's **O** Book
Peter's **P** Book
Quinn's **Q** Book
Rosie's **R** Book
Sofie's **S** Book
Tad's **T** Book
Uri's **U** Book
Vera's **V** Book
Will's **W** Book
Xavia's **X** Book
Yola's **Y** Book
Zach's **Z** Book

* All titles also available in bilingual English/Spanish versions.

WEBSITE
www.dingles.com
E-MAIL
info@dingles.com

My **Letter** Library

S s

My Letter Library leads young children through the alphabet one letter at a time. By focusing on an individual letter in each book, the series allows youngsters to identify and absorb the concept of each letter thoroughly before being introduced to the next. In addition, it invites them to look around and discover where objects beginning with the specific letter appear in their own world.

A a　B b　C c　D d　E e　F f　G g

H h　I i　J j　K k　L l　M m　N n

O o　P p　Q q　R r　S s　T t　U u

V v　W w　X x　Y y　Z z

S is for Sofie.

Sofie is a **s**miling **s**heep.

On Sofie's farm
you will see **s**napdragons
growing in the sunlight,

S s

a shiny **s**axophone

for making music,

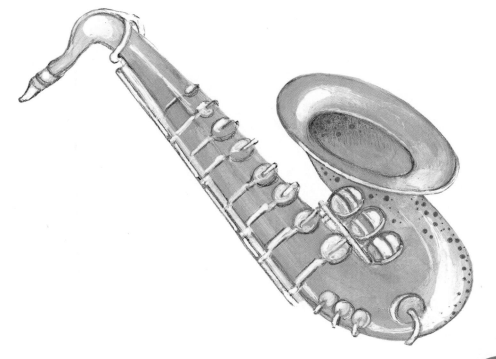

Ss

and **s**lippers

that Sofie's sister

gave her to wear.

S s

While visiting
Sofie's farm you can
pick some **s**trawberries,

S s

sip a cup of steaming soup
that Sofie made,

Ss

or share

some homemade **s**weets

on a plate.

Ss

When walking around

Sofie's farm

you might spot

a **s**nake slithering by,

Ss

a slow-moving snail
named Sam,

S s

and a sticky **s**piderweb.

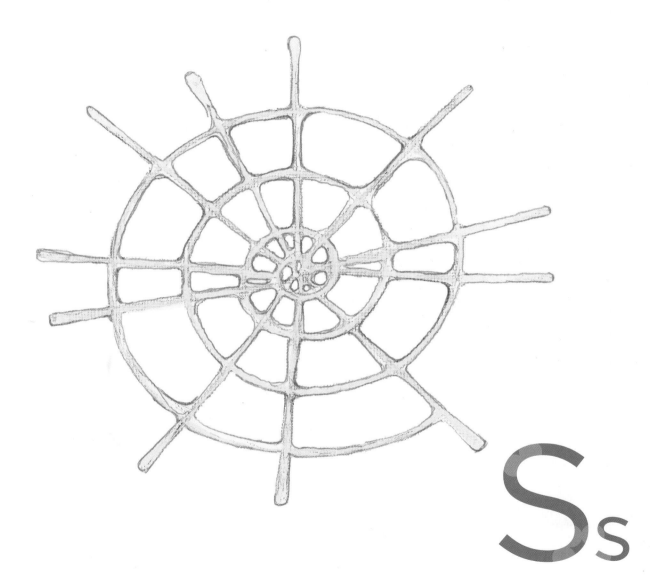

Ss

Things that begin with
the letter **S** are all around.

SNAPDRAGONS

SAXOPHONE

SLIPPERS

STAWBERRIES

SOUP IN A CUP

SWEETS, PLATE

SNAKE

SNAIL

SPIDERWEB

Where on Sofie's farm
can they be found?

Have an **"S"** Day!

Read "S" stories all day long.
Read books about snakes, sheep, slippers, strawberries, and other **S** words. Then have the child pick out all of the words and pictures starting with the letter **S**.

Make an "S" Craft:
Silly String Painting
Choose several colors of tempera paint and pour some into separate bowls.

Then cut one 12-inch piece of string for each paint color.

Have the child dip the string into a paint color and drag it along a piece of construction paper (the paper can be white or colored). The child can use as many colors as he or she wants.

Encourage the child to use his or her imagination and intertwine the lines, make a pattern, or even try to form an object.

Once it has dried, hang the Silly String Painting on display!

Make an "S" Snack: Strawberry Cake
- Remove the stems from 3 to 5 strawberries and cut the berries into thin slices.
- Cut a slice of a premade angel food cake or a golden loaf cake 2 inches thick.
- Place the slice on a plate and have the child put a layer of strawberry slices on the cake slice.
- Then he or she can put a generous scoop of whipped topping on top.
- Put two strawberry slices on the topping and enjoy the Strawberry Cake!

For additional **"S"** Day ideas and a reading list, go to www.dingles.com.

About **Letters**

Use the My Letter Library series to teach a child to identify letters and recognize the sounds they make by hearing them used and repeated in each story.

Ask:
- What letter is this book about?
- Can you name all of the **S** pictures on each page?
- Which **S** picture is your favorite? Why?
- Can you find all of the words in this book that begin with the letter **S**?

ENVIRONMENT
Discuss objects that begin with the letter **S** in the child's immediate surroundings and environment.

Use these questions to further the conversation:
- Have you ever been to a farm? If so, did you have fun?
- What was your favorite animal on the farm?
- Did you get to pet the animals? Which ones felt soft? Rough? Smooth?
- How many legs does a spider have?
- Have you ever seen a large spiderweb?

OBSERVATIONS
The My Letter Library series can be used to enhance the child's imagination. Encourage the child to look around and tell you what he or she sees.

Ask:
- Have you ever pretended to be a farm animal? If so, which ones?
- How many farm animal sounds can you make?
- Can you move like a snake? A snail?
- What is your favorite **S** object at home? Why?

TRY SOMETHING NEW...
Many farm animals have their babies in the spring. Next spring, ask a parent if you can take a trip to a local farm or petting zoo and see all of the new additions!

J. L. MAZZEO grew up in Middletown, New Jersey, as part of a close-knit Italian American family. She currently resides in Monmouth County, New Jersey, and still remains close to family members in heart and home.

HELEN ROSS REVUTSKY was born in St. Petersburg, Russia, where she received a degree in stage artistry/design. She worked as the directing artist in Kiev's famous Governmental Puppet Theatre. Her first book, *I Can Read the Alphabet,* was published in Moscow in 1998. Helen now lives in London, where she has illustrated several children's books.

LDC - 10/09
12-0
C-2